Love's Conception

A Birthing of Love Poems & Prose

by LaLa DeVille

Everybody Publishing

Love's Conception

Copyright © 2019 by LaLa DeVille

Published by Everybody Publishing

ISBN-13: 978-0-9981571-3-9

ISBN-10: 0-998-1571-3-9

Printed in the United States of America

Cover Design by Brijhan Irby

Love's Conception

FOREWORD

When I first met Ms. LaLa, she was an outraged, fist-clenched-and-waving, Chuck-Taylor-sporting Compton disciple whose mission was to let the poetry community know how bad the world is, and how bad it had been to her. But somehow, I still saw a softer, loving side inside. I am now a witness to the transformation that has taken place, just as a caterpillar does after a cocoon stage turns it into a beautiful butterfly. She is now spreading her wings, if you will, after the healing of an angry, crippling past has finally allowed the stretching-out of her creative limbs to express love, admiration, and compassion.

Her growth as a poet has spawned this eye-opening body of work, and hopefully the telling of her experiences will open a few eyes left swollen by the crying that life's griefs has a tendency to throw our way. She is one with a beautiful spirit, whose intentions are always to be helpful. So, she has chosen to take us on a literary love roller coaster, which consists of a series of ups and downs, twists and turns, as well as smiles and cheers. She has poured her personal feelings into these pages, and hopefully it will change your negative outlook on love and spin it into a positive, euphoric experience that you will want to relive over and over again. Please enjoy this poetic rebirth of Ms. LaLa DeVille, as I have.

—Smooth One, The Poet

A real man knows a real woman

when he sees her

and a real woman knows a real man

ain't afraid to please her

> *and a real woman knows a real man*
>
> *always comes first*
>
> *and a real man just can't deny*
>
> *a woman's worth*
>
> *—Alicia Keys*

For Bernard:

Thank you for motivating me to

move my pen in a different, more loving direction.

DEDICATION

I dedicate this body of work to the poets who inspire me to be great. Jaha Zainabu, Donny Jackson, and Father Amde Hamilton, I thank you for teaching me how to walk in the shadows of your greatness.

I dedicate this body of work to all my poetry brothers and sisters (far too many to name) who have supported me on this poetic journey. To my ride-or-die folks, "Smooth One," Renee "Kooki" Chatman, Derek D. Brown, Kuahmel Soul Brother #7, and Charlene "Hustle Diva" Green—thank you for always having my front and my back, in my darkness as well as my light.

PRETTY

I felt pretty wearing

the smile you gave me

You didn't give me pretty

you brought it out of me

Showed me beautiful

because it was me

that your eyes longed

to behold

Many moons it seems

since the last time

I let these magic slippers

caress my gentle feet

and there was something

in my spirit that

asked me to

Just for you

I let down the hard wall

of my exterior and

revealed the softer side

of my vulnerable rainbow

These heels make me

feel pretty enough

to show you how I woman

I be thin framed

long-legged

soft touch

just for you

so take your time

to pleasingly enjoy me

It's been a while

since I felt this way

like Queen worthy of King

No King has ever

been worthy of this Queen

at least not until this day

The day that you made me

feel pretty

INTENTIONS

Before we go any further
I have to ask you this question
I do not want to be out here looking foolish
by assuming and second-guessing

I don't want a repeat
of all the pain I've endured
I need clarity in knowing
if your intentions for me are pure

Now you're already familiar with
the backdrop of my turbulent history
My inner scars run deep; my psyche is damaged
so I don't need anyone adding to my misery

My heart is extremely fragile
the bruise on my spirit is still quite tender
which makes it hard for me to decide
whether or not to you I should surrender

Should I take this leap, step out on faith
and allow myself to fall
or would I be better off walking away
not taking this chance at all

I'd like to remain optimistic

by not thinking all men are the same

from the looks of my past, all I seem to have met

were those into playing mind games

                I accept the fact that they didn't break my heart

                      they failed to meet my expectations

                          now I must take precautions

                  to not find myself in the same situation

I am a woman who now knows her worth

I have no desire to be a man's side piece

I'm quite stingy with mine when it comes to my man

you can't be loving no one else but me

                I'll never ask for fairy tales and make-believe

                  or want for things not within your reach

                      grown women seek something real

                  while little girls believe in a fantasy

Those are some of the reasons I'm asking

if your intentions are genuine and true

If not, I need you to tell me now

so I won't waste my time investing in you

ADDICTED

You are soaked into the pores

of my skin and

braided into the fabric

of my follicles

       You must have put that

black-man magic on me

cuz now I'm feeling

doped up and addicted

anxiously searching for you

all day and all night

       You administered something

and that something is

floating in my veins

leaving me strung out

causing hallucinations

that I have no desire

to withdraw from

I'm jonesing

for another hit of you

to calm this fire inside me

hydrate my wanting for you

that leaves my body inebriated

        This love hangover I have

from the consumption of your

sweet love got me all twisted

I can't think straight no more

        Got me turning left

when I'm supposed to turn right

Got me up all night creeping

when I should be in bed sleeping

Got me itching and scratching

reaching for things

that ain't even there

Baby, your potion has me so

spaced and dazed

I don't know whether to

scratch my watch

or wind my ass

       I don't want no intervention

ain't interested in no rehab

because this addiction is

too strong to shake

and to be honest

I don't even want to try

       I got a habit for you

and it's reeling out of control

So come…

inject me with that good-good

that gets me higher than kites

after swinging lower than sweet chariots

I felt like Saturday in his arms

well received

Welcomed after anticipating

the arrival of me

His hands felt like Sunday

as he stroked my bare skin

baptizing his fingerprint

in the holy waters of my

soft rose-gold stain

If there's a Jesus in the heavens above

this man had me praying to Him

thanking the gods for sending him

on this day

He is my Monday

slow yet necessary

He blessed me by

naming me his next

four days of wanting

and if he could

he would create 365 more days

to accommodate how many

more days he needed to love me

If it were possible

he would remove the weekends

because he never wanted the

week to end

360 degrees of 365 days of love

is what he wished to have

to cherish every second of

every minute of each day

Around midnight

I can hear the turn of your key

in the lock of my door

I'm wrapped in the warmness

of jasmine-scented sheets

as the flicker of a candle's flame

dances wickedly inside the dark

I feel the presence of you

as the smell of your masculinity

floats in the room

Quietly you undress

while my heart flutters

in anticipation

 I have thought

about this chance

for us to wade in

the passion of

each other's reverie

I smile as you slide

in between the sheets

with me

pressing your body

against my back

I love the subtle kisses

you place on my neck

My flesh welcomes

the touch of your hands

caressing my hips

I don't remember ever

desiring a man the way

I thirst for you

However, I'm thankful

that I don't

so I have nothing

or no one to

compare you to

I can feel the heat

stirring between

my soft thighs

The firmness of

your manhood awakens

calling for me

to give myself to you

Hands move behind me

to touch you

to give you permission

to take me…all of me

You turn me to face you

offer me the wetness

of a kiss

while cupping

my breasts with care

You let your tongue

abandon mine

so you can

taste my skin

from my neck

to my stomach

all the way down

to my garden

You proceed to part the gates

open me up

and it is there you

discover my budding flower

I lustfully in my mind

call you my honey bee

because you take pleasure

in drinking in my nectar

where you intoxicate

your sense of thought

Once you complete

your mission

you bring yourself to me

You enter the delectable

part of me

as I taste the orgasm

I left upon your lips

We become tangled

in a web of our extremities

locking fingers

holding hands

bracing ourselves

for the rise to the top

of our peak

where we then free fall

arriving together

at the same time

to the threshold of

our ecstasy

I get so womanly weak

each time you come to love me

turning the key to the lock

to religiously tantalize

my spiritual being every night

around midnight

EARGASM

We exchanged words

through a kiss

savoring the luxurious

taste of each other's

passionate thoughts

His vernacular stimulates

my hungering ears

as my poetic dialect

makes love to his

THE LIPS OF A POET

(our first time)

Have you ever

      kissed the lips

           of a poet

Have you ever

      felt as if your body

fell into the core

           of ecstasy

EASY

I may appear foolish
But I do wish
I could spend my days
With you

        In so many ways
        I do want to say
        These feelings I have
        are definitely true

        I can't lie
        nor will I deny
        I would die
        Should you ever
        Leave me

                No one ever said
                falling in love
                would be easy

I was Queen Humpty Dumpty

who fell off my walled throne

far too many times

Leaving the shell

of my existence cracked and

damaged beyond repair

They said I could not be

put back together again

but this beautiful Mahogany King

believed otherwise

He was wise enough to know

anything was possible when it came

to finding his Queen

and no mere tear nor fracture would

keep him from loving her

He slowly approached the puddle

of hurt that surrounded her

giving deep thought

as to how he could lovingly arrange

the shards and create her anew

into beautiful blessing she once was

He wiped the one tear

that rolled from her grieving eyes

placed a soft kiss upon her forehead

and gently picked up

the fragments of her heart

the jagged edges of her soul and

remnants of her broken spirit

He held each piece close to his heart

closed his eyes and wished a prayer

to the universe asking for the strength

of his heart to resurrect his newfound

Queen back to life

Back to a life where he could

love her through anything

if she would trust him

enough to let him

Her heart began to awaken

came alive in just a few minutes

wanting to live life again in his presence

He vowed to love her pain away for always

and place the world at her feet

the Mahogany King didn't

need his horses

and King's men to help him

for he put Queen Humpty Dumpty

back together all on his own

LIBRARY

Read my lips

continuously

Learn them by heart

as if they were

 your favorite poem

Write my wrongs

with the precision

of a felt-tip pen…smoothly

Translate my body language

with your eyes

so you can understand me

I want your tongue to

speak me

into the existence

of your universe

Make me a chapter

in the book of

real love

never turning the pages

Your loyalty to me will

be the bookmark

I need to make sure

you never lose

your place

with me

no matter how much

you study me

I will never test your patience

Plagiarize my

feelings for you

erase you from

my table of contents

and you'll be my bible

because I'll always believe in you

THE LIPS OF A POET

(sweetness)

I kissed a poet

I tasted the

honeysuckle

sweetness of

a soliloquy

waiting on the

tip of his palate

I savored each

love poem that

dripped from his

patient lips

Kissing him again

and again so my lips

could hear it once more

I touch parts of myself

I have reserved for you

as my fingers slide into

my personal inkwell

My fantasy of you

leaves its fingerprints

in my thoughts

I don't consider that

as being self-pleasure

I consider it wishful thinking

…of you

NAKED

He stripped me...naked

stripped me of my insecurities

exposed my vulnerability

while peeling away layers

of my decayed pain

He desired to see me free

of all doubt that covered my heart

Longing to relieve my mind

of the negative vices

I had grown so

heavily dependent upon

He yearned for me to bare all

Urged me to eliminate

myself of anything not designed

to comfort me

His mission was to

show me how beautiful

I was underneath the garment

of my unhealed wounds

Unravel the lies others

maliciously tucked away

in the hem of my spirit

Once my scars were unsheltered

shame was no longer

a jaded accessory to complement

the tattered fabric

I became accustomed to

I was now open to the elements

of honest love

ready to clothe myself

in the love he customized

to fit only me

PRELUDE

(after we kissed)

It was then
he chose to
cocoon himself
inside the folds of
my pulsating walls
where he loved me
like it was to
be his last time
I let the tips of
my delicate fingers
read the smoothness
of his back as
we kissed again
reciprocating each
other's passion
letting my soul
drink him in
while I quenched
his thirst

His lips spoke

my climactic finale

into his here and now

where we became one

All of this from

nursing the

curiosity of

kissing a poet

He doesn't mind

letting the world know

that I am his

and I don't mind

letting the world know

he is mine

Now there is a difference

between keeping

your business to yourself

and keeping your commitment

a secret

You see

he moves in silence

Still waters run deeper

than bloodlines

while I am ocean current

better yet tsunami

but that's alright

because he understands

my storm

my thunder

and he respects it

 I never try to convince him

to move to make waves

simply because I do

In dark shadows he watched me

not in that stalker-like way

but in a way where

he studied me

Evaluating my actions

memorizing how the pain

and anger looked on me

Biding his time

to make his move

to prove he had

done his homework

all while I was living out loud

Still hurting, trying to

pretend I wasn't

He saw through me like glass

and recognized I was

a scared little girl deep down

that created a tough exterior

to provide the protection

no one else had

the nobility to do

REASON

I am not the easiest pill to swallow

Who told you to love me

and all my flaws?

Who asked you to

penetrate the thick skin

that confined my cries and

who informed you to

let me know it was okay to breathe?

I've been scuff-marked

and drenched in a

dystopia of pain

baptized in the burning hell

of mistreatment

then left to crawl and claw

my way out of a bucket

full of crabs that kept

pulling me back to where

I used to be and

back to the wounded bird

I once was

My ragged flesh was

full of prickly thorns

I bled profusely over

everything around me

but then you found me

wrapped your arms around me

and gave me one of the

greatest things next to life itself

You gave me a reason

An unconditional reason

to just be

Be beautiful

Be fabulous

Be phenomenal

hell, be bold, courageous

and unapologetic

You gave me a reason

to smile at the reflection

of myself that I was

once afraid to lay my eyes upon

Gave me a reason

to feel no guilt

anytime I began to

believe in myself

You gave me a reason

 not permission

 to be the best woman

 best poet and

 best lover I could be

 Reason came accompanied

 with hope, joy, and smiles

 More laughter than

 one soul could contain

 and more love than

 one heart could hold

 That's why I chose to

 share it with you

 So you can experience

 what your reasons

 have done for me

 Your reasons gave me

 motivation to do all the things

 others told me I could not do

It was your reasons

that kept me from

convincing myself

someone else out there

is much better than me

With every reason you provided

I repetitively saw your smile

because your happiness

is also a reflection

of my happiness and

that is the most remarkable thing

anyone could ever witness

I don't know who it was

who told you to love me

and all my flaws

I don't know who asked you

to penetrate the thick skin

that confined my cries

or informed you to

let me know it was okay to breathe

but whomever it was

I'm glad they gave you a reason

to do that for me

SAFE

His arms were a safe place for me

Cocooned in blissful warmth

manifested by his admiration for me

I have awaited this moment

since my last lifetime

even though I had no idea

I was actually waiting

He made me feel safe

ready to open my heart

and receive him

rest my head on the

pillow of his compassion

as his tender and gentle heart

massaged mine whole once again

I closed my eyes

and felt him breathe life

into the cracks of my soul

unblind me to see

how beautiful love

with him could be

We lay quietly

as he allowed me

to peacefully die

so when I awakened

I would be reincarnated

into that past life

that now lives

Vicariously inside

his spirit

Together we are now one

Spiritually connected

as extremities

prove that love

has infinite gratuity

THE LIPS OF A POET

(the experience)

When I kissed a poet

I felt parts of me tremble

I never knew existed

His desire for me

anticipated

my crave for him

dissipated

SUNRISE

As I watch the sunrise

I think of you

It's the representation of

another day anew

The warmth is the Creator's smile

and all its glory

Birthing the next chapter

in our love story

Does the sunrise make you

think of me

as you drink in and bask

in all its beauty

I anticipate the dawn each night

as I close my eyes

because I love you even more

with every sunrise

THAT KISS

He had me at that first kiss

working magic, putting a spell

on my soul

our lips softly brushed

our wanting desires

we kissed feverishly

we touched the epitome

of our tender

He touched parts of me

that his palate craved

tasted the spice of my garden

that flourished a waterfall

that left him intoxicated

punch drunk off wine

made from the yearn

of my crying orgasm

"I love you" makes him nervous

Fearful of the inevitable

I, however, am not

afraid of the word

Just afraid of losing us

So we won't tell one another

"I love you"

we'll just simply say

"I got you"

Love Quote

(I want to save time with you)

Sometimes I

cease to

breathe

Pretending it will

allow

time to stand

still

so the togetherness

we share

can last a few more

infinities

LOVE SONG

Every time I hear

a silly love song

it reminds me of you

how you bring me joy

when you do the things you do

There'll never be another

man who could ever

take your place

I know that you have love for me

cause it's written

all over your face

Anytime and anyplace

if you need me

I'll be round

Don't look any further

'cause I'll be the one who'll

hold you down

I'm not gonna lie

I just wanna be your girl

Let me open up my heart

so you can share my world

So anxious to do

a little sumpin' sumpin'

Come around my way

'Cause I need your lovin'

When I'm with you

you keep making me high

you know this love is real

'cause kisses don't lie

It's alright if you choose

to settle for my love

any amount of love you give

is never too much

I'm not going to ask

what took so long for you

To walk into my life

I already know the answer

The Creator had to take me

through some thangs

so I could find my value

buried underneath

the sticks and stones

meant to break my bones

He took me through some thangs

so I could see past the blindfold

that kept me from laying eyes

on what I knew was of no good to me

Why did I need to see

when it felt so good

but over a timespan

I discovered what felt

good to my body

was dismantling my spirit

He took me through some thangs

so I could learn my voice

use my voice to speak up

and speak out to demand my respect

tell my testimony

become spokesperson

for the reflections of me

who too needed the key

to unlock their cage of courage

I was forced to swallow bitter

pills and foolish pride

feed on the ingesting

of my own truth

then purge myself to freedom

New woman clean

able to clearly recognize

her beautiful grains of life

giveth to me to plant for manifesting

the best life and right love

that had been out there

Creator had to take me

through some thangs

and I know why I endured it all

being sacrificial lamb

He took me through some thangs

to better prepare me

for the arrival of you

LOVE QUOTE

(astronomy)

He is the moon

To him I am sun

He never ceases to show up

I never cease to brighten his life

I promise to give you all of me

every ounce of my heart, soul, and loyalty

Since the day we

discovered one another

the sun appears to rise quite differently

The moon shines much brighter

and every star in the sky you

reach for it

hand it over to me

because the universe told you

they were God's diamonds

He created to be forever mine

What you have brought to my life

has begun to slowly

break down the wall

around my heart I put up to protect it

because you have lovingly

taken the broken shards

into your hands to help

piece them back together

Your love and genuine respect

have removed all doubt

all past growing pains

and for us I'm ready

ready to replace the old with new

I want to grow with you

spiritually

I want to be there for you

emotionally

and you have shown me

that you too desire to join me

in building that foundation for us

If all that I've faced in my life

was the blueprint

that led me to you

I'd have to honestly admit

it was well worth it

It taught me that real men

who honor real women

Look like you

and love the way you do

I want to be everything beautiful

to you

while you be the right man

that came into my life

at the right time

to love, cherish, and behold me

in the right way

VOODOO

The secrets from his lips

convinced my body

to spread my thighs

like rumors

> I lay back
>
> enjoying the feel of his smile
>
> splashing in the tide
>
> of my tsunami

His crave awakened

black-magic orgasms

that burst into

the creation of white lightning

> The soil inside my earth
>
> was then moistened
>
> growing love within
>
> from the root
>
> he placed upon me

We are not just

hot sex on cold nights

Sweat-drenched bodies

on love-soaked sheets

nor are we

flowing streams of ecstasy

we both concur to dive in

         We are friendship first

              lovers second

          Deep discussions and

      belly laughs that conceive tears

We have become

newfound joy

each other's confidant

He, my pillow of rest

Me, his saving grace

We're foot massages

and head rubs

Next to God

> he is my everything
>
> He is my God
>
> and me, I be his Goddess
>
> Together we be everything

The imprint of his devotion

stains the walls of my mind

For every time he swims

inside my love, poetry is born

Our simplicity will always

 nurture our creations

never to abandon our

childrenated love poems

Each time I reflect on

The object of our intimacy

I feel chills massaging

the smoothness of my skin

just like he does when he

desires to be next to me

As we make love

my orgasms appear like waves

inside the hemisphere of my being

What has this beautiful man done to me?

Is this a dream or is this

what real love looks like?

It feels as if my body is

featherlight as I fall

float, then land on a bed of roses

Feels like we're walking on water

holding hands that are

meshed into one

For every lover of my past

who found time to neglect me

He found time to bring transparent beauty

to the threshold of my heart

Yes, the tunnel to my heart was dark

but he was not afraid to enter darkness

to rescue the remaining piece

of love left for me to give

He was aware my well of love was running dry

But he offered a replenishment

no other man desired to give

As we lay

skin to skin

Caressing

Conversing

Holding

Touching

Loving

Laughing

Fingers exploring me

tongue sampling you

as I swallow your inner thoughts

You fascinate me

I excite you

We be each other's muse

Pen me

Paper you

Transcribe experiences of

our documented emotions

and notarized togetherness

I love you

You love me too

www.ingramcontent.com/pod-product-compliance
Lightning Source LLC
Chambersburg PA
CBHW071415170626
46811CB00003B/1415